a Fragile inheritance

a Fragile inheritance

The care of stained glass and historic glazing: a handbook for custodians

Sarah Brown and Sebastian Strobl

CHURCH HOUSE PUBLISHING

Church House Publishing
Church House
Great Smith Street
London SW1P 3NZ

ISBN 0 7151 7600 5

Published 2002 for the Council
for the Care of Churches by
Church House Publishing

Copyright © The Archbishops'
Council 2002

Typeset in Sabon 11pt

Printed in England by ArklePrint
Ltd, Northampton

Contents

Illustrations

Acknowledgements

The authors have benefited from the advice and support
of their fellow members of the Council for the Care of
Churches Stained Glass Advisory Committee: Dr Tim Ayers,
Dr Alexandrina Buchanan, Dr May Cassar, Martin Harrison
and David O'Connor. The assistance of the Council's
Conservation Officer, Andrew Argyrakis and Conservation
Assistant, Dr David Knight, has also been invaluable.

Introduction

Stained glass is one of the most compelling forms of church decoration, and yet it is also one of the most vulnerable and least understood. It is subject to degradation as a result of its chemical composition, and it is vulnerable to the elements. It has also been attacked by religious iconoclasts, removed as a result of changing taste, and been all too often the target of malicious damage and vandalism. Nonetheless, many churches retain vestiges of the medieval glazing that was once one of the great glories of the English parish church. Far fewer churches preserve windows of the seventeenth and eighteenth centuries, by which time the traditional craft had been subject to a technical transformation. For the vast majority of churches, it is the rich inheritance of the neo-Gothic stained glass revival of Queen Victoria's reign that now requires care and maintenance. Whatever the date of the window, stained glass enriches, enhances and illuminates the church interior, and England can boast a national heritage of exceptional richness. It is an inheritance of great diversity, including the medieval treasures in the parish church of Fairford in Gloucestershire, the seventeenth-century delicacy of the enamel-painted glazing of Lydiard Tregoze in Wiltshire, the Victorian splendour of the Morris & Company windows at Brampton in Cumbria and the twentieth-century vibrancy of the Marc Chagall windows at Tudeley in Kent, to name but four examples. Many churches also preserve historic plain glazing, expanses of mouth-blown glass manufactured in a time-honoured tradition and full of the imperfections, idiosyncrasies and visual interest that give the glass a character unmatched by industrially manufactured materials.

This guide is designed for those entrusted with the care of this fragile inheritance: clergy, congregations, churchwardens, architects, parish fund-raisers, Diocesan Advisory Committee (DAC) members and their advisers. It is intended to serve as a brief guide to the causes of the deterioration of stained glass and an introduction to the steps involved in commissioning professional advice and thereafter to managing the conservation and future care of this valuable resource. Please note that no work should be carried out to the windows in your church without first obtaining a faculty. Contact the Diocesan Advisory Committee or your archdeacon for advice.

Stained glass conservation is a relatively new profession. It has emerged from an older craft tradition in which the repair of a weathertight window was the primary concern, often irrespective of the spiritual, historical and artistic qualities of the window. In recent years, however, the profession has been evolving rapidly, working closely with professional and heritage bodies such as the Council for the Care of Churches (CCC), the British Society of Master Glass Painters (BSMGP) and the United Kingdom Institute of Conservation (UKIC) to develop high standards of good practice. This has coincided with a period of sustained research and investigation into the physical and chemical properties of stained glass and its environment. One aim of this guide is to assist the custodian in the assessment and interpretation of the specialist reports that are now provided. Conservation can be expensive, so it is important to ensure that the right strategy has been chosen for the care of the windows in your church. In many cases, however, sensible and often inexpensive 'good housekeeping' will ensure that your windows enjoy a long life. Above all, this is a guide for the non-specialist!

Sarah Brown and Sebastian Strobl

chapter 1

'Let there be light': historic glazing in the English parish church

'Let there be light': with these words God initiated the creation of the world described in the Old Testament; in the New Testament Christ is described as the light of the world. A material that could illuminate a building while preserving its occupants from inclement weather was highly prized indeed, and it was this symbolic significance that helped to transform the prosaic craft known to the Romans into a Christian art form. Coloured glass, arranged in a lead framework and enhanced with the surface application of a painted pigment, flooded the church with light and could provide an illuminated narrative of religious and devotional imagery.

Archaeological finds and literary evidence reveal that the great cathedral and abbey churches of Christendom were being glazed with figurative windows from the sixth and seventh centuries. The earliest stained glass surviving *in situ* in great English churches, the cathedrals of Canterbury and York, dates from the second half of the twelfth century. The evidence for the use of painted glass windows in English parish churches in the same period is far less plentiful. A simple figure, probably of St Michael, in the parish church of Dalbury in Derbyshire may be the earliest surviving stained glass (perhaps of the early twelfth century) in an English parish church. Its narrow proportions suggest that it was made for a single lancet opening above an altar. Windows above altars were probably the primary ones for which stained glass was provided, particularly the east window over the main altar, where the Crucifixion and the saint or saints to whom the church was dedicated were often the commonest subjects depicted, as at St Agatha's, Easby, North Yorkshire.

fig. 1
Thirteenth-
century plain
glazing of
unknown
provenance. The
design depends
on the limited
amount of
coloured glass
and the strong
lead lines. The
leads are
substantially
original.

Other windows in churches may have been filled with simpler forms of glazing: geometric patterns with no paint and sparing use of colour, or unpainted diamond quarries of clear glass. Thousands of parish churches still preserve old quarry glazing of medieval or early modern date, fashioned out of hand-crafted glass, but many more churches have lost this beautiful material to careless or uninformed restorers. Despite these losses, interesting examples of historic plain glazing survive in The Stained Glass Museum in Ely (fig. 1), at the parish churches of Hastingleigh and Brabourne in Kent and at Marston in Oxfordshire. Efforts must be made to ensure that there are no further losses, and that experienced conservators are trained to recognize historic plain glazing as well as more conspicuous stained glass.

Stained glass became far commoner in the parish church in the thirteenth century. The introduction of plate-tracery, and subsequently bar-tracery, created larger, more decorative and complex window openings and afforded the glaziers' craft greater prominence. The increasing importance of devotion to the saints, especially the growing devotion to the Virgin Mary, reflected in texts such as Jacobus de Voragine's *Golden Legend*, came to be expressed increasingly in stained glass, either in the form of single figures or as narrative cycles of scenes arranged in medallions or geometric frames. The emerging theological concept of purgatory and the consequent belief in the efficacy of the intercession of saints provided an additional impetus, while belief in the power of the intercessory prayers of the living was responsible for the burgeoning fashion for donor commemoration in stained glass. One of the earliest depictions of a donor figure in English stained glass was in the parish church of Upper Hardres in Kent, where Philip and Salomon de Hardres were depicted before the Virgin and Child in a window of c.1250, since destroyed by fire.

The years around 1300 saw the transformation of the architectural context of stained glass windows, as the miniaturized architecture of shrines and tabernacles began to be reflected in their structure. The simple two-dimensional structures sheltering figures at the parish church of Selling, Kent (c.1299–1307, see fig. 2), were succeeded by the sort of three-dimensional canopy structures seen at both the churches of Eaton Bishop and Moccas in Herefordshire (c.1330–40). The Selling windows also incorporate recognizable naturalistic foliage and a display of heraldry, a means of commemorating benefactions, marriages and dynastic and political alliances. In the early-fourteenth-century chancel of Norbury parish church in Derbyshire, the side windows contain a display of heraldry set into silvery grisaille with no figurative glass.

fig. 2
The Virgin and Child and saints under simple canopies, set into painted grisaille with heraldry. The east window of St Mary the Virgin's Church, Selling, Kent, c.1299–1307.

At the same time an important technical innovation, the use of a silver-nitrate pigment commonly called silver stain or yellow stain, further transformed stained glass. The yellow stain was applied to the exterior surface, and turned white glass a silvery or an orangey yellow when it was fired. The technique considerably reduced the need to cut and lead small inserts of glass and was used extensively to colour hair, beards and small details of clothing and drapery. The stain could also be used to achieve green when applied to blue glass.

By the fifteenth century, stained glass had become one of the pre-eminent forms of church decoration. The parish churches of medieval cities such as Bristol, Coventry, London, Norwich and York were filled with pictured windows, resplendent

fig. 3
Feeding the hungry, one of the corporal works of mercy. East window of Holy Trinity Church, Tattershall, Lincolnshire, glazed by the workshop of Thomas Wodshawe and Richard Twygge, c.1480–82.

with images of Christ, the Blessed Virgin Mary and the saints, together with images of those men and women whose wealth had helped to pay for the churches and their decoration. The wealth of the urban rich was reflected in a new range of moralizing and instructive themes in windows, including the depiction of the corporal works of mercy: the virtuous use of earthly riches spent in the acquisition of spiritual credit. In All Saints, North Street, York (c.1420–30), and Tattershall in Lincolnshire (c.1480–82, fig. 3) the good deeds are performed by a man, while at Guestwick in Norfolk (c.1460–80) they are performed by a woman. Merchants' marks and cyphers joined the heraldry of the gentry as a means of identifying donors.

In the course of the fifteenth century, better quality white glass became available, together with an increasingly diverse range of imported coloured glasses. Ruby (red) and blue, two of the most expensive colours, were used in profusion, often in counter-changing combinations, with expanses of sparkling white enlivened with silver stain. The importation of richly brocaded fabrics from the Orient is reflected in stained glass quarry designs and in the increasingly sumptuous textiles depicted in windows. A taste for richly jewelled surfaces was expressed in stained glass by the insertion of glass 'jewels' into hems and crowns, such as those surviving in late-fifteenth-century glass at the church at Stockerston in Leicestershire.

In the last quarter of the fifteenth century immigrant glass-painters began to arrive in England, attracted by valuable commissions from royal, aristocratic and ecclesiastical patrons. Coming from the Low Countries (modern-day Belgium and the Netherlands), they brought with them the exciting realism admired in panel paintings. In 1497 Barnard Flower was appointed glazier to King Henry VII, the first foreign artist to achieve this coveted post. Teams of Anglo-Netherlandish artists were entrusted with the most prestigious projects of the day, including King Henry VII's new Lady Chapel at Westminster Abbey, St George's Chapel, Windsor, and the chapel at King's College, Cambridge. Their work is also to be found in a number of parish churches, including West Wickham in Kent, Kirk Sandal in South Yorkshire and St Michael and All Angels Thornhill in West Yorkshire, and in the 28 astonishing windows of St Mary the Virgin, Fairford, Gloucestershire (see fig. 4). While the patrons at West Wickham, Kirk Sandal and Thornhill all had aristocratic and court connections, John Tame of Fairford was not an aristocrat but a member of a wealthy merchant class, aspiring to greater social status and with vast resources at his disposal. Stained glass was becoming a powerful status symbol.

But just as stained glass was achieving new heights of technical and artistic sophistication, political events were transforming the

fig. 4
The head of a Christian martyr (c.1500–15), north nave clerestory (window NII), St Mary's Church, Fairford, Gloucestershire. This detail reveals the remarkable virtuosity of Fairford glass-painters.

medieval world. King Henry VIII broke with Rome over the issue of his divorce and remarriage, aligning England with the Protestant Reformation. While the extent of the destruction of religious imagery in parish churches resulting from the Reformation has probably been exaggerated, the dissolution of the monasteries between 1536 and 1541 resulted in much being destroyed. Some parishes benefited from the closure of their monastic neighbours; the parish of Wing in Buckinghamshire, for example, bought a stained glass window from the abbey of Woburn, while the parish church of Morley in Derbyshire preserves the late-fifteenth-century cloister windows from Dale Abbey. In the reign of the young

King Edward VI (1547–53) superstitious images in church windows were specifically prohibited for the first time. The market for new stained glass, as for other forms of ecclesiastical art, collapsed.

However, the high cost of reglazing a parish church meant that the destruction of the sixteenth century was often sporadic and sometimes confined to the breaking of heads and removal of only the most sensitive of subjects. A far more serious threat was to be gradual decay and neglect. As the making of stained glass declined, few skilled craftsmen remained to undertake repairs, which were entrusted to plumbers.

Stained glass enjoyed a short-lived revival in the seventeenth century. In the reigns of James I (1603–25) and Charles I (1625–49) churchmen anxious to restore the seemliness of worship were in the ascendant, and the installation of stained glass was tolerated, if not encouraged. The most influential churchman was William Laud, Archbishop of Canterbury from 1633 to 1645. The archiepiscopal palace chapel at Lambeth was filled with new stained glass, and at his trial in 1644 Laud was charged with 'countenancing the setting up of images in churches, church-windows and the places of religious worship'.

The stained glass artists of the seventeenth century were working in new ways. Not only were their designs heavily indebted to continental pictorial sources, popularized by prints and engravings, but they also emulated the styles of easel painters, using some traditional pot-metal glasses but also relying on the wide range of vitreous enamel pigments now available for colouring white glass. The college chapels of the universities of Oxford and Cambridge and the chapels of the Inns of Court preserve some of the finest collections of these enamel painted windows, but parochial examples survive in the churches of Lydiard Tregoze in Wiltshire and Abbeydore in Herefordshire.

This revival was cut short by the outbreak of the Civil War in 1642. In the years that followed, stained glass suffered attacks far more serious than those caused by the Reformation. Stained glass in the cathedrals of Worcester, Lichfield and Peterborough was despoiled by parliamentary troops, although in York the parliamentary commander, Sir Thomas Fairfax, forbade the destruction of windows in the Minster or parish churches. In East Anglia the enforcement of parliamentary directives against superstitious images was entrusted to the Puritan William Dowsing. Many churches lost their statuary, screens and windows to his fanaticism, gleefully recorded in his journal.

Following the restoration of the monarchy in 1660, stained glass was no longer subject to government prohibition and the attack of religious zealots. However, a more dangerous foe was widespread artistic indifference to the medium. The prevailing architectural fashion, baroque classicism, had little place for painted windows. Stained glass did not cease to be made, but it had been reduced to a minor craft.

The eighteenth-century Romantic movement found new inspiration in the arts of the medieval past, and the revival of interest in stained glass contributed to the craft's survival. Antiquaries and collectors such as Horace Walpole (1717–97) and William Beckford (1760–1844) admired the architecture and decorative arts of the Middle Ages, and in their houses, Strawberry Hill and Fonthill, they employed contemporary glaziers to make new windows and to create sympathetic settings for fragments of old glass, often collected on the Continent. Small decorative pieces, notably silver-stained roundels, were imported in large numbers. For Roman Catholics like Sir William Jerningham of Costessey Park in Norfolk, stained glass was a means of recreating a pre-Reformation devotional atmosphere in a private chapel.

During the long reign of Queen Victoria (1837–1901) the thin trickle of new stained glass commissions became a torrent. By the end of the eighteenth century, classicism was being challenged for architectural pre-eminence, a battle of styles from which Gothic would emerge triumphant. A decisive moment came in 1834 when the competition to design the new Houses of Parliament was won with a Gothic design by Sir Charles Barry (1795–1860). The young Roman Catholic architect Augustus Pugin (1812–52), champion of the Gothic Revival, was employed to assist Barry in the execution of the buildings, which were provided with richly coloured stained glass windows made in the medieval mosaic tradition. For Pugin the ecclesiastical

Gothic style (see fig. 5) was far more than an aesthetic preference; it represented the reclamation of the Church from pagan classicism. The revival in stained glass benefited from the great surge in church building in the nineteenth century. Cities such as London, Liverpool, Birmingham and Manchester grew enormously, attracting an influx of people seeking work in their dockyards, workshops and factories. The majority of new churches built to accommodate the expanding urban populace were in the Gothic style.

The transformation of stained glass production in the first half of the nineteenth century can be gauged from the Great Exhibition of 1851. Twenty-five firms exhibited stained glass, in a variety of antiquarian styles from the twelfth century to the seventeenth. The recovery of medieval-type pot-metal glasses, thanks to the researches of the glass historian Charles Winston (1814–65), was a further advance. These new 'antique' glasses provided Victorian glaziers with materials that closely resembled those of the medieval masters whose works they admired and sought to emulate.

By the 1860s the production of stained glass had achieved something like industrial proportions, with scores of studios in London and at least one studio in most major provincial towns. The major studios of Clayton & Bell, Heaton, Butler & Bayne, and Lavers, Barraud & Westlake were all founded in the 1850s, with Morris, Marshall, Faulkner & Company (later Morris & Company), Burlison & Grylls and C.E. Kempe following in 1862, 1868 and 1869 respectively. The younger generation of artists, notably William Morris (1834–96), Edward Burne-Jones (1833–98; see fig. 6) and Henry Holiday (1839–1927) brought a new vitality and creativity to stained glass, with designs indebted to the art of the medieval past but not slavishly in thrall to it.

A desire to break free from increasingly industrialized manufacture underpinned the philosophy of the Arts and Crafts movement and its pioneer Christopher Whall (1849–1924). Whall worked independently of the commercial studio system and became the most influential stained glass designer and teacher of his generation. While his undoubted masterpiece

fig. 5
St Ethelbert.
Panel designed by
Augustus Pugin
and executed by
John Hardman,
ca. 1850. South
nave (sVIII, 2a),
St Augustine's
Church,
Ramsgate, Kent.

is the glazing of the Lady Chapel of Gloucester Cathedral, his
work can be seen in numerous parish churches, and his influence
was disseminated widely through the Central School and Royal
College of Art in London, the Birmingham School of Art and the
Dublin Metropolitan School of Art. His influence was also felt in
Scotland and the USA. Arts and Crafts studios provided exciting
opportunities for women designers and makers of the calibre of

11

fig. 6
The east window
of St Martin's
Church, Brampton,
Cumbria, with
figures designed
by Edward Burne-
Jones, made in
1880–81 by the
firm of Morris
& Company.

Veronica Whall (1887–1970) and Wilhelmina Geddes
(1888–1955; see fig. 7), barred from working in the male-
dominated commercial studio system. The philosophy of
the Arts and Crafts movement remains a powerful force in
contemporary stained glass in Britain, and the medium
continues to attract many women artists.

In the twentieth century two world wars fuelled demand
for commemorative windows, many of them in a traditional
figurative style that was beginning to look outdated compared
with the abstraction and expressionism of other painted media.
In the post-war years two great cathedral-building projects,
Anglican Coventry and Roman Catholic Liverpool, provided
showcases for modern stained glass design, both introducing a
mixture of figurative and abstract forms, and a combination of
traditional and modern techniques. While it is unlikely that the

fig. 7
The Deposition
of Christ,
east window
of 1922,
St Luke's Church,
Wallsend, Tyne
and Wear, by
Wilhelmina
Geddes.

number of church windows commissioned in the twenty-first century will ever approach the numbers made in the nineteenth, the glaziers' art continues to flourish, and many new Millennium windows have now been added to our stained glass inheritance.

chapter 2
More than just glass

A historic window is far more than just an expanse of glass. Even the simplest window of unpainted diamond quarries represents the efforts of a skilled craftsman. A stained glass window represents the collaborative efforts of a designer, a cartoon maker, a glass-cutter, a painter and a glazier, and many windows require the skills of a blacksmith to make the iron framework (the *ferramenta*) which supports the glazing within the window opening. Every component of the window may contain valuable information concerning historic glazing techniques and craftsmanship. A conservation programme should respect and seek to preserve as much original historic fabric as possible, and should address the care of all aspects of the window and its architectural environment.

Glass

It goes without saying that the principal component of a window, whether stained glass or decorative plain glazing, is glass. Its main ingredients are silica (sand), alkali fluxes (potash or soda) and often colouring agents (in the form of metallic salts). The heating and fusing of these ingredients combine them into a malleable, fluid material that when heated sufficiently can be blown into vessels, or discs or sheets suitable for glazing. Glass is a relatively brittle material, and its chemical composition makes it vulnerable to atmospheric pollution and to moisture. Pot-metal glasses are of a single colour. Flashed glasses are made by applying a layer of colour to a white or coloured base; 'ruby' (red) on white is the most commonly found flashed colour. The surface colour can be abraded away or acid-etched to create two colours on a single piece of glass. From the sixteenth century onwards, a striated glass (often called 'Venetian') was made by trailing coloured glass onto the surface of a clear sheet. This glass is a rare occurrence in English windows. The artists of the Arts and Crafts movement of the late nineteenth and early twentieth centuries favoured a slab glass, made by blowing it into a rectangular bottle mould. These 'Norman slabs' are of uneven thickness and give their windows a particular brilliance. Sparkling whites, jewel-like and streaky colours, and a sumptuous and costly gold-pink are characteristic of the finest windows of this period.

All mouth-blown antique glasses have a unique quality and liveliness. Replacement of old glass by new should always be kept to an absolute minimum, whether it be in a stained glass window or in a window of unpainted antique diamond quarries.

The industrialization of glass production in the nineteenth century resulted in the creation of many new, textured, machine-made glasses, frequently used for domestic decorative plain glazing. Many of these glass types are no longer made and so are very difficult to match. It is important that any historic window is entrusted to a specialist conservator able to recognize a wide range of historic glasses and, if necessary, to match lost glass with a material of a comparable colour and quality.

Lead

The second major structural element in any stained glass window or decorative glazing is lead. Lead strips, H-shaped in cross-section and commonly called 'cames' or 'calmes', provide the ideal means of joining together pieces of glass, which are inserted under the 'leaf' or flange of the lead on either side of its 'heart'. Medieval window leads were cast in moulds, with any rough or uneven surfaces planed away to give them a distinctive faceted profile. Since the late sixteenth century, lead cames have been made by extruding the lead through a mill. It was common for these lead mills to impress a maker's name and sometimes a date into the heart of the lead, thus providing valuable historical and dating information. Many books continue to state that window lead has a life span of only one hundred years. While

fig. 8
The medieval lead matrix removed from the Jesse Tree window of Canterbury Cathedral (corona nIII). The outline of the enthroned Virgin Mary can still be clearly discerned in the lead outline, underlining the closely integrated nature of the relationship between glass and lead.

it is now believed that milled leads may be weakened by the milling process, it is certainly not the case that windows always require releading after a century. Part of the late-twelfth-century Jesse Tree window in Canterbury Cathedral (corona nIII), for example, remained in medieval lead until 1953 (fig. 8), and many of the early-fourteenth-century choir clerestory windows of Cologne Cathedral remained in their medieval leads until the 1960s. The medieval east window of Gloucester Cathedral was re-leaded in 1861–2, and shows no sign of requiring releading in the near future.

The lead cames are an integral part of any stained glass or decorative glazing design. Different thicknesses of lead will have been chosen to strengthen and complement the outlines of the design. During conservation every care must be taken to identify historic leading, and to retain it if at all possible. If the historic leading has failed and its retention would compromise the safety and stability of the window, it should be examined and recorded carefully, and its replacement should match the original in width and profile. In the case of unpainted glazing, the design will rely entirely on the interplay of glass and lead. Failure to deal with

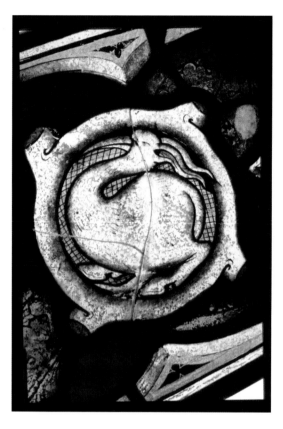

fig. 9
A grotesque creature in the north antechapel window of New College, Oxford, c.1386. Yellow stain has been used to enliven white glass and glass-paint.

this relationship in a sensitive manner can have a disastrous effect on the appearance of a historic window. Any historic lead removed from a window should be preserved.

Surface decoration: paints, stains and enamels

This is the most vulnerable aspect of a window. The decorative or narrative message is enhanced by the addition of painted details, which can be applied to both internal and external surfaces (fig. 9). Glass-paint, black or dark brown in colour, contains iron oxide and finely ground glass. It is mixed with gum arabic to make it adhere to the glass, and can be diluted to an ink-like consistency suitable for strong outlines (*trace lines*) or to provide a more fluid, modelling wash. It is then fired in a kiln, which fuses it permanently to the surface of the glass.

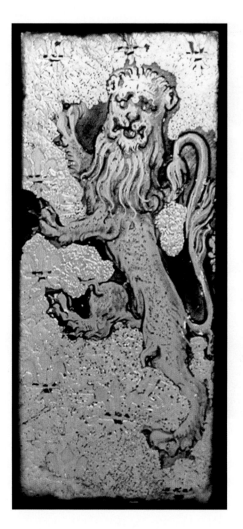

fig. 10
Almost total loss
of blue enamels in
this lion rampant
guardant from the
Hoby Chapel east
window, All Saints'
Church, Bisham,
Berkshire.

From the early years of the fourteenth century a silver-nitrate pigment, commonly called yellow stain or silver stain, was applied to the glass surface (usually the exterior). When fired the stain turns white glass yellow, and blue glass green. Until the sixteenth century, glass-paint and yellow stain were the only colouring agents that could be applied to the surface of glass. In the sixteenth century a new haematite-based pigment, a vitreous enamel called variously *sanguine* and *Rouge Jean Cousin* (after its supposed inventor), began to be used, rather sparingly to begin with. It warmed the colour of glass-paint used to model skin tones, and was applied to lips and cheeks to give them a realistic blush. In the late sixteenth and seventeenth centuries further enamel colours were introduced. They were favoured especially for the decoration of complex and intricate heraldic displays, and were used as substitutes for increasingly scarce supplies of traditional pot-metal coloured glasses. Unfortunately the longevity of these enamel colours is dependent upon accurate firing temperatures, and many enamel-painted windows now suffer from pigment loss (see fig. 10).

Ferramenta and fixing systems

Glazed panels are usually supported in a window opening in the glazing grooves cut into the window jambs. Glazing set into smaller openings, usually at the top of a window, may not require any additional support. The panel will be held firm in the opening with mortar. A small number of panels remain fixed in medieval mortar, which should be preserved whenever possible. If it is impossible to preserve the mortar, it should be carefully recorded. In openings of larger size, glazed panels require additional support, usually in the form of internal saddle-bars and external stanchions (see fig. 11). The glazed panels are fastened to this framework with copper ties. In the twelfth and thirteenth centuries the iron armatures were fashioned into complex geometric shapes that echoed the geometric patterns of the glazing itself. The glazing was then fastened into the framework with iron pegs. The ferrous metal framework, or *ferramenta*, is often an integral feature of the masonry of the window opening, with bars passing through the window mullions. Its maintenance is critical to the stability of the window, as rusting ironwork not only stains the masonry but also expands, causing stonework to fracture and burst. Any conservation project therefore must take the state of the *ferramenta* into consideration.

Some thirteenth-century panels were supported in wooden frames within the window opening, held in place with iron pegs, as at Salisbury Cathedral. Although these frames have often been patched and mended by successive generations of craftsmen, every care should be taken to preserve these historic fixing systems.

fig. 11
Conserved
medieval
stanchions at
St Peter's
Church, Monks
Horton, Kent.

Ventilation

Many windows contain features designed to provide the church
with ventilation. Sometimes this can be in the form of decorative
pierced-lead ventilation grilles, set into the window itself.
Alternatively, opening casements may have been fitted, although
the action of opening these can cause damage to the surrounding
window. If neither form of ventilation has been retained,
alternative provision must be considered. More rarely, some
windows retain vestiges of shutters – a complement, or even
an alternative, to glazing, especially in domestic contexts.

chapter 3

The importance of 'good housekeeping'

Your church is unique in every sense, and so are the windows, which are an integral part of the decoration of the building, regardless of whether they are leaded lights of geometric pattern or artistic stained glass. Getting to know your windows is therefore the first important step in an effective regime to preserve your heritage, and is an essential basis for good housekeeping. Learn as much as you can about your stained glass, and record your findings in an inventory that can be handed on to your successor. The Church Recorders of the National Association of Decorative and Fine Arts Societies (NADFAS) have compiled many such inventories, and one may already have been compiled for your church (see Appendix C).

Such an inventory should include a full set of *dated* photographs, which will provide an unbiased record of the condition of your windows at the time the images were taken. Photograph every window, recording both internal and external surfaces, including the plain glazed leaded lights. None of us can predict what will be of interest to future generations, and a particular feature or an entire window disregarded by our generation may become a focal point for study in years to come.

These images will also help you to monitor any changes in the condition of the windows. Stained glass and leaded lights deteriorate gradually over a long period of time, so you will be unlikely to notice changes on your frequent visits to the church. Refer to the images from time to time, and make them available to your architect, who will find them a useful tool in drawing up the quinquennial inspection report. Sadly, there might also be occasions when you will need a photograph on a much more ad hoc basis. The disastrous impact of vandalism or adverse weather conditions, which might affect your church at any time, will be greatly reduced if you can provide the conservator with good images showing the window before the damage occurred.

How to take these images adequately using conventional techniques is described in more detail in Appendix D. Digital imaging instead of traditional film is increasingly common, and may well be preferred for ease of handling; however, remember that this is still a new technology, and that you will have to check points such as compatibility with new formats on a regular basis. Once the images have been taken, store them in a safe place in the church, along with your other records of church furnishings. It addition, it is essential to store another set of photographs away from the church, to prevent the loss of records in case the building and its content is destroyed by a fire.

Disaster planning is another important step towards good housekeeping. In your action plan you should first address whether there is an immediate need for protection for your windows, and then establish the procedures in case disaster strikes. Assess the security of the environment in which the church is located and keep this assessment up to date. Are the windows exposed to stones thrown up by a lawn mower? Is vandalism to buildings on the increase in your area? If the answer is yes, you might wish to consider the introduction of protective glazing or wire guards. Advice about the systems available is given below (pp. 45–50).

Your inventory will help you to decide which windows to protect first, in case it is impossible, for financial or architectural reasons, to cover them all. But do bear in mind that selective protection inevitably draws attention to unprotected windows. Remember that any kind of protection provides cover only against accidental and casual damage. For those intending to cause serious malicious damage by hitting the glass or by forcing entry into the church, the guards will be a visual deterrent at best.

Your disaster planning should also cover action necessary in case forced entry is required for more benign reasons. In a fire emergency, for example, the fire brigade may need to break through one or more windows. Give some thought in advance, and if necessary seek advice, as to which losses would cause least damage to the historical and decorative integrity of the church. Invite officers from the police and the fire brigade to discuss your damage-limitation plan with you.

Apart from the more obvious threats to the glass discussed above, there are environmental hazards, such as high levels of relative humidity (RH), which lead to condensation on the inner glass surface. Under normal circumstances condensation is easily overlooked, or if noticed is often accepted as a phenomenon which will disappear as soon as the glass warms up. Remember, however, that water is the main catalyst for the deterioration of both glass and paint pigments. Keeping levels of relative humidity inside the church low and as stable as possible is therefore an indispensable part of good site management. Seek advice on adequate heating and, most importantly, keep the church ventilated throughout the year's cycle. In contrast to the Victorians, who made a point of introducing casements in their new windows, we tend to prevent fresh air from entering a church, mainly for reasons of heat conservation. Casements are thus often kept shut, disused, defunct, sometimes even deliberately sealed. Make sure they are working; consult your architect if they are not, and use them.

Last but not least, the cleaning of your church is another important aspect of good site management, aimed at maintaining a well-cared-for interior. However, it is imperative that you advise your church cleaners against dusting the surface of stained glass windows. Paint pigments might have become unstable and could thus come off at the slightest touch. Sweeping away cobwebs should therefore be confined to cills and window reveals. The problem of excessively dirty windows is addressed in Chapter 4, but in any case seek professional help if you feel your windows require cleaning.

chapter 4
When to call in professional help

The emergency

A glazing emergency can arise at any time, often overnight or at a weekend. It is therefore advisable to have prepared a plan of action in anticipation, which will allow you to respond promptly and appropriately. Storm damage is a continuing problem. Hurricanes in 1703 and 1987 both caused considerable damage to weakened church windows, unable to survive sudden wind-pressure of exceptional force. Sadly, deliberate and malicious damage by vandals is all too common a problem in both urban and rural parishes, while windows continue to be a favourite point for breaking into, (or out of), locked churches, which causes damage to painted and unpainted windows alike (see fig. 12). Find a local contractor experienced in dealing with historic buildings and able to board up a damaged window at short notice. This will not only enable you to act immediately but will also ensure that emergency 'first aid' does not make the situation worse.

On discovering a damaged window:
- Photograph the damage immediately. This will assist both your insurer and your conservator.
- Collect *all* fragments of broken glass, no matter how small. Check cills and the ground both inside and outside the church. Taking great care, remove any loose or dangling fragments in danger of falling out of the window. *Do not* use adhesive tape to hold together any broken pieces, as this can remove painted pigment.

fig. 12
The aftermath
of a break-in:
Trinity Methodist
Church, Romford,
Essex, May 1997.

- If for reasons of security and weatherproofing it is necessary to have a damaged window boarded up, ensure that the task is entrusted to a contractor used to working in historic buildings. No boarding-up should be installed by drilling into the stonework, nor should any large holes be made good by a large sheet of glass being attached to the surface of the historic window with a silicon adhesive.

- Contact your insurer immediately. If the damage is extensive, inform your architect, who will assist in commissioning conservation assistance.

'Tell-tale signs': recognizing signs of potential danger

The results of vandalism or storm damage are by their nature easy to spot. Much more difficult are the detection and correct interpretation of other, more subtle signs of the gradual deterioration of your windows. As always, when in doubt call in professional help, ideally in consultation with your architect. But there are signs which you will find easy to recognize and, within reason, to act upon – or carefully assess whether action is needed, as by no means every problem requires immediate or urgent attention.

Apart from the buckling of panels (see below, p. 31), the most common signs of developing problems are water stains on the cill and on the wall beneath the window (fig. 13). In all likelihood this staining means that the window in question is leaking in severe weather conditions. If this is the case, you will have to act very soon in order to avoid serious damage, not only to the window itself but also to the masonry, which will cost your parish dearly to put right. But before jumping into action, check first whether the seepage persists or has come to a halt. Monitor the window on rainy days and look for wet spots on

fig. 13
St Michael's Church, Heydour, Lincolnshire: wall and cill badly stained by water seeping through a leaking window.

the cill, or for water running down the stone surrounds and the glass, easy to detect under surface light produced by a torch. In extreme cases you may find that the staining is caused by excess condensation, which means you will have to find ways of reducing the humidity within the church. Either way you will need professional help, so call a conservator and describe your observations, as it may not be possible for the conservator to verify the causes when they visit the church.

In most instances, however, excess condensation does not manifest itself in the build-up of larger droplets and wet cills. If the conditions are conducive to condensation, a fine layer of water will form itself on the surface of the glass as soon as the temperature outside the church falls below that of the inside. Surface accretions, such as organic growth, will start to appear, first on a microscopic level, but before too long detectable by the naked eye and possibly affecting both the internal and the external skin of the glass (see figs 14 and 15). A greenish layer is a sure sign that you will have to act, as microbes cause damage not only to the corroded surfaces of medieval glass but also, in the longer term, to otherwise sound new glass.

fig. 14
St Michael's Church, Heydour, Lincolnshire: build-up of surface accretions and rusting *ferramenta*.

fig. 15
Organic growth
on the internal
surface of the
east window of
Little Malvern
Priory,
Worcestershire,
c.1480–82.

However, do not wait for this green film to appear on the glass. Recurring condensation can also endanger the paint pigments, in many cases long before infestation by microbes becomes noticeable. Paint pigments on stained glass, often described as vitreous paint, may become unstable and lift off for a multitude of reasons, but their deterioration is sometimes triggered and always accelerated by excess water. The resulting 'ghost' images, where the loss of paint lines has created a reversed positive–negative impression or even blank spaces, are a common occurrence on medieval glass as well as in many Victorian windows (see fig. 16). When you see this phenomenon in one of your windows, do not try to assess the condition of the

fig. 16
Ghost' images
left by the loss
of original
painted detail
on a Ward &
Hughes window
of 1866 in St
Martin of Tours
Church,
Ashurst, Kent.

remaining paint layers yourself, for example by scratching over the surface with an instrument or your fingernail. Once removed, paint pigments are lost for ever, so leave every step beyond mere visual inspection to the conservator.

For the same reasons, you should not attempt to remove cobwebs or wipe over 'excessively' dirty windows. It is often difficult to tell what this 'dirt' consists of and what lies underneath. Occasionally the layer of 'dirt' may be a varnish of cold paint applied in a deliberate attempt to tone down the window, possibly for artistic reasons. Or it may be a mixture of dust and other particles carried by the air and bonded together on the glass surface by condensation. Nor is the occasional splash of emulsion paint dropped onto the glass during the last decoration of the internal walls unusual. Whatever this layer consists of, its removal would take any loose pigments underneath with it, and it is therefore the experts' task to decide on the most appropriate way forward, which might well be not to touch the window at all.

You may find that some glasses in your older windows have darkened so much that their translucency is all but gone. Sometimes this darkening might have developed within the

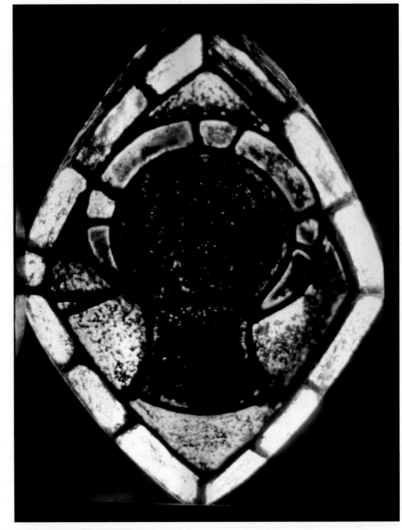

fig. 17
A thirteenth-
century head of
Christ in
window nIII, St
Mary's Church,
Denton, Kent,
now completely
obscured by
the irreversible
browning of the
medieval glass.

body of the glass itself, a process which is called browning
(fig. 17). Mostly, however, you will find a whitish layer on the
external surface of the window, a sure sign that glass is in an
advanced state of corrosion. Browning is a process that can
be neither halted nor reversed, but it does not endanger the
physical existence of the glass. Corrosion, on the other hand,
ultimately leads to its destruction (see fig. 18). In the latter
instance you will find that the conservator will recommend
action which goes far beyond the mere cleaning and possibly

fig. 18
Corrosion crusts on the exterior of medieval glass in the tracery lights in the south chancel (window sIII), All Saints' Church, Odell, Bedfordshire.

the removal of the corrosion crust, in order to bring the process to a halt. If this is the case, ask for a detailed condition report which will help you and others to understand the implications of the proposed conservation measure. Chapter 5 will give you an insight into what to expect from such a report.

Another well-known and often reported phenomenon is the buckling of panels and sometimes of entire lights. Buckling or bending is a matter of concern, but it by no means always requires immediate attention. On close inspection you will find that many of your windows buckle slightly anyway. Movements caused by the daily cycle of heat expansion and contraction, or by the downward pressure created by the panels' own weight, are an inherent occurrence and might have come to a halt a long time ago. Only beyond a certain degree does buckling begin to affect the structure of the panel and cause harm to its component parts. If the panels are buckled but still as firm and stable as they were on day one of their manufacture, the window might be better left untouched for many years to come.

Ultimately it is the conservator who should decide whether action is necessary. Signs to look for, however, are movement under wind pressure which means that the panels in question

fig. 19
Copper tie detached from the lead came of the panel, taking a strip of lead with it, thus creating a hole in the matrix of the Burne-Jones east window of 1876 at St Michael and St Mary Magdalene's Church, Easthampstead, Berkshire.

have indeed become unstable. Also, have they lost their connection with the structural support system, such as the internal saddle bars or the external stanchions? The copper wires soldered onto the panels and tied to the bars might be torn off and are thus not functioning any longer (fig. 19). Has the buckling created undue stress on the glass, which might cause it to fracture along the lines of the movement? When any window reaches a certain age you should expect a number of fractures within it. These do not require attention unless they are severe, for example star cracks, but do look out for this particular problem. Has the buckling advanced to a degree where individual pieces of glass begin to stand proud of the lead matrix or possibly even begin to fall out? Can you see daylight coming through? Then it is time for action.

You might also be able to see daylight between glass and the lead matrix, or even between panels and the stone surround, for another reason. If subsidence has caused the wall to move, the fracture may run through the window itself. Depending on the strength of the mortar used for the pointing of the panels, a gap can appear between the panels and the glazing grooves, or the panels may be ripped apart along certain lines within the lead matrix. Your architect will highlight these problems in the quinquennial report, but if you have noticed evidence of this problem do not wait to get confirmation in writing. The panels in question could have become unstable, and picking up the pieces after a storm will be much more expensive than any proactive preservation measure, not to mention the considerable loss of historic material that might have resulted.

Last but not least, have a good look at the mullions and stone rebate close to the structural support bars of the window and monitor both on a regular basis. In all likelihood the bars will be of ferrous metal, which might have started to corrode heavily and, depending on the quality, to laminate. The expansion of the metal set off by this lamination will have a negative effect on the masonry, fracturing the stone which holds the bars in place (see fig. 25). Look out for the signs of this particular damage. Fractures in the stone close to the ironwork mean that you should immediately call in an expert, who will be able to advise you as to the urgency of the problem.

chapter 5

What you can expect from a conservator

The detailed condition report

If a window in your church has sustained extensive damage, or your windows are displaying the signs of deterioration described in the previous chapter, the commissioning of a detailed condition report is an essential tool in the successful management of a conservation project. It is common practice to invite more than one studio to tender for any significant programme of work. Indeed, competitive tendering may be a requirement of your insurer or grant-giving body. Your chosen contractors will provide a condition survey as part of their conservation report and proposal. However, you may prefer to commission a separate specialist condition report as a first step. In it the conservator will provide you with information on the condition of your windows and make recommendations for their conservation independently of the tendering process.

There are a number of advantages to this approach: first, you will be separating the assessment of the conservation requirements from the costing issues, bringing clarity to the early stages of the conservation process. You may, of course, receive the good news that your windows are in a sound state and require no immediate conservation. Second, if the report reveals that conservation is required, you will have a document that can be supplied to those conservation studios invited to tender for the project, providing the basis for an objective tendering process on which you can judge costed proposals. Be aware, however, that other conservators may have a different perspective on the problems encountered and may reserve the right to comment accordingly. Finally, the condition report will be an invaluable tool in the fund-raising efforts which are essential for all but the richest parishes. Whichever route you adopt, be prepared to pay for a thorough specialist report.

It is a sound investment: the more information you have assembled at the outset, the better placed you will be to make informed decisions about the conservation and preservation of your windows.

Appendix A contains the format for a condition report as recommended by the Council for the Care of Churches, the British Society of Master Glass Painters and the United Kingdom Institute of Conservation Stained Glass Section. It is a format familiar to specialist conservators and indicates the sort of topics and level of detail you should expect to see.

In summary, in the condition report, the conservator will:
- Identify the date and/or artist of the glass
- Identify conservation problems
- Assess the underlying causes
- Evaluate their seriousness
- Provide advice on the urgency (or otherwise) of remedial work
- Outline a range of conservation options and offer recommendations as to the most appropriate

It is important to choose a conservation studio with the right kind of expertise for your windows. Appendix C contains addresses of those organizations able to provide information on specialist conservators and restorers.

Monitoring and understanding the environment

The condition report will provide you with all the information required to take appropriate action for safeguarding the future of your windows. While this report will concentrate on the windows, it may also contain recommendations regarding the local environment surrounding the glass and possibly covering the entire building. Climate control within the church is an integral part of good housekeeping, as discussed in Chapters 3 and 4, and over recent years monitoring of the environment has thus become increasingly important in the preventative conservation of the glass, helping you to recognize potential problems before they turn into real ones. For example, in consultation with your architect, establish that the heating system suits not only the churchgoer but also the building itself. The dangers of high levels of humidity have already been discussed, and they affect not only the glass but also all furnishings and the entire fabric. Therefore, being able to read the signs, to understand their origins and consequences, will reduce the need for intervention later on, saving not only historic material but also money. So familiarize yourself with the issues at stake and ask your architect or the conservator in charge what you can do to monitor the situation. In exceptional circumstances, monitoring equipment may be required to obtain the necessary information, but it will be for your architect to assess the need for this in co-operation with the conservator.

Understanding the conservation proposal

It is the architect's responsibility, in consultation with the Diocesan Advisory Committee (DAC), to advise you and to ensure that the right conservation studio has been chosen for the project. The architect and conservator then need to advise whether further technological studies and scientific analysis are to be carried out to form the basis of a conservation concept. While you may therefore assume that the conservation proposals are appropriate and indeed the best way forward, it is nevertheless up to you to read the proposal carefully, to understand its implications and, if necessary, to question its recommendations. Guidance on the requirements to be met by a conservation report, against which you can measure the particular proposal you have received, can be found earlier in this chapter (see pp. 34–5).

There are certain fundamental principles which should underpin all conservation proposals, and it will save you a lot of time, administrative work and money if you check that your conservation proposal conforms to these standards before you begin. But whatever you decide to do, remember that the risks involved in removing a window for conservation may sometimes outweigh the benefits. Ask the architect and the conservator for their assessment of the possible problems arising from the removal of the glass, and satisfy yourself that you can establish a consensus which will help you to justify any subsequent steps.

The overriding principle underpinning modern conservation is that of minimal intervention. The over-rigorous approach of past restorers has taught us that even the best-intentioned interventions can easily lead to unnecessary loss of valuable

fig. 20
The miraculous draught of fishes, Corpus Christi Chapel (sV), St Mary's Church, Fairford, Gloucestershire, c.1500–15. The original figure of Christ and much of the background of the first light has been badly damaged. The late-seventeenth-century restorer has carefully recreated the figure of Christ, and has used the surviving details in the second light to recreate the cityscape in the background.

historic material, which includes lead and ironwork. The extent of replacements in a vandalized panel, or any rearrangement to 'correct' previous restorations, must therefore be carefully considered before any action is taken, as earlier restorations are themselves part of the history of the window (see fig. 20). The aim should always be the preservation of the maximum amount of original historic fabric, which is easier to achieve in the case of stained glass than in, for example, stone conservation, where, for reasons of structural safety, original stone may have to be replaced. The permanent removal of stanchions, however, is totally out of the question.

The principle of minimum intervention and maximum preservation of historic fabric necessitates the application of reversible conservation techniques. Surface coatings are therefore not admissible. You should question the conservator if the specification proposes the repainting and refiring of original glass, as this process in effect destroys its authenticity and integrity as a historic object. Ask for a full specification of all conservation materials to be used, as their application and long-term properties have similar implications.

The best specification comes to nothing if the conservator in charge is not competent to implement it. Check, via your architect or DAC, if appropriate, on the conservator's qualifications, and make sure that you ask whether any part of the work is going to be subcontracted. Visit the studio while work is in progress. This is not only an excellent opportunity to see the glass at close quarters but the craftspeople in the studio will also appreciate your interest in their work.

Finally, check the specification for the extent of the documentation the conservator is intending to provide. In many cases it will be sufficient to record a replacement piece by taking a photograph only and by signing the piece with the initials of the conservator and the date of the restoration. Before and after conservation photographs should, in any case, form the basis of every repair or restoration work, but as a matter of good practice, and not only when required for grants, all work beyond a straightforward releading or *in situ* replacement should be recorded on diagrams and annotated

fig. 21
Lower part of the figure of David, north nave window (nlll), St Germanus' Church, Faulkbourne, Essex, 1920. Repair lead above the ankle of the right foot follows the line of the lace to disguise the insertion of a replacement glass. The left foot remained undisturbed.

rubbings and in written documentation, such as a final report, depending on the extent of the work (see Appendix B).

A conservation proposal will suggest a variety of conservation methods, based on the condition of your window. The following list is by no means exhaustive – and cannot possibly be so, since every project is unique and thus requires a fresh approach – but it aims to provide you with an insight into the most common techniques you might encounter when reading the proposal or visiting a studio.

Fractured glass: mending techniques

In line with the principles of minimal intervention, fractured stained glass of any age should be retained as long as its preservation can be justified on structural and technical grounds.

● The traditional, albeit the most intrusive, way of mending broken glass is by the introduction of repair leads (see fig. 21). Their flanges are usually quite narrow in order to reduce the visual impact, but they still require the removal of some original glass to make way for the hearts of the H-shaped cames. Repair leads should therefore be a technique of last resort.

- A less intrusive and visually more pleasing effect is achieved by the use of copper foil. Best known for its use in Louis Comfort Tiffany's (1848–1933) elaborate windows and lampshades, the self-adhesive copper foil is attached to both edges created by the fracture. The two pieces can thus be soldered back together again, which creates a bond between them and leaves only a thin strip, marking the line of the mended crack.

- The visually most pleasing effect is achieved by the use of adhesives such as silicones, acrylic or epoxy resins (see figs 22 and 23). However, with the exception of silicones, the use of which is restricted for other reasons, most of these adhesives are not designed to last in an unprotected environment. Unless further protection measures, such as isothermal glazing, are introduced as part of the conservation process, the use of copper foil is thus the best compromise between structural necessity and visual appearance.

Cleaning: benefits and methods

The reasons for removing surface accretions are obvious and in most instances fully justifiable. Dirt reduces the enjoyment for the onlooker, while microbial growth such as algae is harmful to the glass. However, a decision to remove the weathering crust on the glass itself in order to improve the transmission of light is much more questionable, and may easily lead to over-cleaning if carried out by an inexperienced person. Putting aside the fact that the crust is part of the historic fabric, albeit transformed over time, its uncontrolled and complete removal will lay bare the sound body of the glass, initiating further corrosion. Even the most detailed site survey cannot establish an appropriate way of cleaning the glass, and in the preliminary assessment no report should, therefore, propose anything more than cleaning with deionized water. Further cleaning techniques, such as the use of glass-fibre brushes and high pressure air, can only be considered after detailed assessment in the studio.

fig. 22
Late eighteenth-century portrait of Queen Anne, St Mary the Virgin and St Hugh's Church (nVI, 4d), Old Harlow, Essex, before conservation, with the head of the queen disfigured by mending leads.

fig. 23
The portrait of Queen Anne after conservation, with disfiguring mending leads removed and the fractured pieces edge-bonded.

fig. 24
Paint loss as a result of moisture attack in the form of condensation, clearly visible on the interior surface of the glass. Little Malvern Priory, Worcestershire, c.1480–82.

Consolidation of paint pigments and leadwork

Over time, paint pigments can become unstable and, as a result, may detach themselves from the body of the glass onto which they had initially been fused. Under normal circumstances you will notice this condition only when a certain degree of paint loss has already occurred (see fig. 24). If this is the case, you may assume that some of the remaining paint pigments will require consolidation as part of a major conservation and protection project, but it is important that the specification refers only to those areas where the pigments are loose and detached and not just unstable. This is necessary because consolidation of loose pigments with the techniques currently available is irreversible, and the long-term effects of the materials used cannot be predicted with certainty. Unstable pigments which still adhere to the surface should therefore be left untouched, as other protection measures are designed to take care of their material survival.

Another important component of any panel is the lead. For many centuries this was regarded merely as a structural support to the glass, without any artistic or other merit of its own. Only in recent decades have we come to realize not only that dismantling of panels exposes the glass to unnecessary stress and danger of breakage, but also that lead has its own historic value and is an integral part of the original design. As the structural element of the panel, lead is subject to different principles of preservation than glass, and the same can be said of the surrounding stone. But the common assertion that lead needs replacing every hundred years or so is a misconception. More often than not, buckled panels can be straightened again and broken solder-joints can be mended. Partial releading can save much of the original leadwork. A complete dismantling and disposal of the old lead should only be considered when an assessment on the bench reveals further problems within the lead matrix. You should question any proposal for complete releading which is based solely on the statement that the window is buckling.

Ferramenta and structural support

In the past the structural ironwork in a window, described as saddle-bars, *ferramenta* or stanchions according to their design and use, has been regarded as a sacrificial accessory and has thus long shared the fate of the leadwork. Even today stanchions, for example, are often seen as 'in the way' when it comes to the introduction of new stained glass windows, particularly when the new design has not taken their existence into account.

Any proposal, be it for conservation or the introduction of new stained glass, must include an appropriate specification for the retention and the treatment of the metalwork. This should include derusting, priming and top-coating of the bars. Depending on the quality of the metal, the specification might also include the cutting-off and replacing of the ends with non-ferrous metal to prevent corrosion and subsequent lamination of the iron, with its well-known detrimental effects on the masonry (see fig. 25). Internal support bars should receive the same treatment as their external counterparts.

fig. 25
Rusting saddle-
bar bursting
masonry, St
John's Church,
Tunbridge
Wells, Kent.

However, you will find that most conservators recommend the replacement of low-quality Victorian saddle-bars with non-ferrous metal bars. As an exception to the general rule this may be acceptable, as the retention of these saddle-bars will in the long term compromise the condition of the glass panels and their architectural surrounds.

Masonry

Stained glass is an art form which relates closely to the architectural environment for which it was designed, becoming an integral part of the building in which it is installed. By implication, therefore, a window can only function properly in aesthetic terms while remaining *in situ*, and its long-term survival depends decisively on the condition of its surrounding masonry or other framework, including the entire wall.

A condition report for a window should therefore always include an assessment of the architectural surrounds. You cannot expect a stained glass conservator to give recommendations for stone conservation, so where there are obvious signs of deterioration of the stone the report should include a referral to a specialist in this field. Even if there are no apparent problems at this stage of commissioning the conservation of a window, you should make allowances for unanticipated masonry problems. Especially in older stone, there is a chance that faults are hidden under the mortar, or that an intricate tracery is held in place only by the rigidity of the glass panels. For this reason it is common practice for architects to include in their invitations to tender a contingency sum for additional stone repair. By following this good practice you will guarantee that you have enough funding at your disposal to ensure that the masonry will be ready to receive the conserved window on its return, and that the stone will serve the window for many years to come, thus avoiding the need to remove the window again solely for the purpose of stone conservation.

The return of the window – protection

Glass is an extremely fragile material and does not therefore naturally lend itself to use in a hostile environment. However, its unique properties of translucency have resulted in its use as a weathershield for more than two thousand years. In the case of stained glass it has also served for many centuries as a form of artistic decoration. This dual purpose has made stained glass vulnerable to both mechanical and environmental damage.

A newly conserved window is as deserving of protection against this hostile environment as any other window in your church, perhaps more so. Whatever the reason for the removal of the window for conservation, as custodian you will want to guard against future damage from whatever source. The protection of a window is consequently an integral part of its conservation, and must be taken into consideration at the outset of any project. Do not, therefore, accept any specification which lacks an assessment of the causes of damage to the window and recommendations to prevent their reoccurrence.

Protection of the window should obviously be geared towards the special requirements of a particular window. Is there a real danger of vandalism, or has the window suffered from the ravages of time and weather? Answers to these questions will determine whether your window needs protection from mechanical damage only, or whether more far-reaching environmental protection is required. Generally, windows made prior to the Victorian age will need

fig. 26
Staining of the
external cill
caused by
leaching of salts
in the copper
window grilles,
St Mary's Church,
Patrixbourne,
Kent.

the latter, whereas for 'younger' windows a more traditional means of protection may suffice, although here too environmental protection is sometimes necessary. Equally you will need to consider how the window protection will affect the appearance of the building as a whole.

Protection from 'mechanical damage' – wire guards and protective glazing
The protection of windows is usually initiated as a result of mechanical damage, caused by external impact such as vandalism or storm damage. The traditional way of overcoming this problem is by the installation of wire guards, for centuries made from ferrous metal or copper. The Victorians, in particular, provided their windows with this safeguard, but these older guards are today quite often heavily corroded and offer little protection.

Indeed, the salts coming out of the metal may stain the cill and mullions a deep brown or green and cause extensive damage (see fig. 26). Check your existing guards, and have them removed if necessary.

If you are satisfied you need guards, the modern solution is black powder-coated, stainless-steel wire guards, manufactured to fit into each individual opening of the window, leaving all masonry fully exposed. In most installations these guards are unobtrusive and hardly visible on the outside of the building. They do, of course, show on the inside, depending on the design of the window or the intensity of the daylight, but they are often a necessity and the lesser of two evils.

Wire guards will protect against most kinds of mechanical damage, but there is a limit to what can be achieved. A greater degree of protection is provided by external protective glazing, most commonly in the form of sheets of polycarbonate. However, owing to both their impact on the visual appearance of the exterior of the church and their short life, you will find it difficult to justify their installation (see fig. 27). The mirror effect created by the sheets will spoil the prospect of the external elevation of the church, even if they are cut to the shape of each opening – a minimum requirement if you were to apply for a faculty granting their installation. A costly but aesthetically preferable alternative might be the manufacture of leaded lights of an appropriate design, to be installed as the external protective layer.

A stained glass specialist will be able to advise you on the options available, in both the use of materials and the design of the protection, and also to help you make a case to your DAC. Heat conservation, for example, cannot be used for justifying this measure, although this factor undoubtedly would be a beneficial side effect.

Environmental protection – isothermal glazing
Sometimes glass requires protection not only against vandalism but also from the elements. In an architect's or a conservator's specification you will therefore notice that medieval windows in particular, may be subject to the introduction of an isothermal

fig. 27
Mirror effect on
external poly-
carbonate
sheeting, St
Wandregesilius'
Church, Bixley,
Norfolk.

glazing system. If isothermal glazing is suggested in a proposal,
ask the conservator to explain the reasons for this course of action.

Atmospheric pollution and microbial growth, but most of all
the mere presence of water in the form of condensation or rain,
are the main catalysts for the degradation of glass and paint
pigments. Once this process has set in there is no conventional
means of stopping the deterioration, which progresses at an
ever-increasing pace. If an assessment of the condition of a
window has identified such degradation, or the clear danger of
its onset, action is imperative. The principal aim must be to
relieve the stained glass of its function as a weathershield by

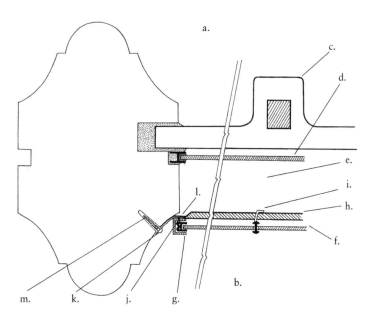

fig. 28
Cross-section of an isothermal glazing system: a. Outside; b. Inside; c. Original lugbar; d. New kiln-distorted protective glazing; e. Internally ventilated inter-space; f. Original stained glass; g. 10 x 10mm MB4 frame; h. Support bar; i. Copper tie; j. Copper rivet; k. Bronze fixing bracket; l. Leaf-lead light shield; m. Brass screw.

creating a physical barrier towards the environment, and only an internally ventilated protective glazing system, usually introduced while the glass is removed for conservation, can provide this. The removal of the glass gives an opportunity to mount the historic panels in purpose-made bronze frames, which are subsequently fixed to the inner edges of the window apertures while the protective layer of clear glass is fitted into the original glazing grooves (fig. 28). The bronze frames are provided with lead flanges which fit tightly to the masonry, leaving only a few gaps at the bottom and top of each light for air to enter the interspace between the protective and the historic layers to prevent moisture from being trapped there. As the air is drawn from the inside of the building, a glass temperature equal to the room temperature is achieved, and condensation will not usually occur on the glass. The provision of an equal temperature gave the system its name, isothermal glazing.

The introduction of an isothermal glazing system may appear at first too interventionist, as its installation affects the appearance of the window both internally and externally. A proposal for its introduction is therefore sometimes met with concern. However, research is continuing into its effects on the building, and new information may come forward. Installed correctly, and provided the internal environment is taken into account, the isothermal glazing system has minimal effects on the glass and the masonry; the process is largely reversible in the event of a less interventionist solution being found in the future.

Every window installation is unique, and therefore the decision on its protective glazing and its design must take into account the particular preservation needs of the stained glass and its architectural setting as well as the physical and aesthetic impact on the building (fig. 29). A stained glass specialist will be able to explain these needs to you. In discussion with the architect, the conservator may provide you with a proposal for an isothermal glazing system tailored to the requirements of your window, balanced against the requirements of other parts of the fabric. The introduction of an isothermal glazing system will reduce the extent of interventionist conservation treatment to the glass, thus saving not only historic material but also your parish some money, now and in the longer term.

fig. 29
Late-fifteenth-century donor figures in window nXXII in Long Melford Church, Suffolk. The lower part of the window is protected by the installation of an external isothermal glazing system; the upper half remains unprotected.

A specimen condition report

The Church of England
Council for the Care of Churches

Guidelines for minimum information required in conservators' reports accompanying faculty and grant applications

Part A: Preliminary Report

Stained Glass

1. Location of stained glass
Use the Corpus Vitrearum Medii Aevi System or a diagrammatic plan. The CVMA numbering system is preferred. If another system is used it must indicate the precise location of the windows. A ground plan should always be included.

2. Description of the window opening
i.e. number of main lights and dimensions. A measured sketch is acceptable.

3. Description of stained glass
Give date, artist, identification of subject, details of inscriptions, if any and bibliographic references, if appropriate.

4. Photographs
These should be good quality colour prints or colour photocopies of the interior and exterior. All images to be annotated with dedication and location of building, window number, light number, panel number and date. There should be general and detailed views, to show the condition of the window/s. Points of particular relevance should be highlighted.

5. Condition of glass

This should include all related materials, the glass, pigments, paint/enamel, stain, masonry, brick, lead, structural supports, the materials of any protective system that may be in place and the type and size of the structural support. It should also include details of any previous restoration or conservation programmes.

6. Conservation proposals

The conservator should outline all the options for conservation treatment indicating which of these is his/her preferred option and why.

7. Estimate

The preferred option should be costed and the date until which this is valid should be given. VAT should be shown separately and should be included in the total cost quoted.

A specimen conservation report

The Church of England
Council for the Care of Churches

Proposals for the Conservation of Stained Glass

Part B: Record of Conservation

The information provided in the preliminary report covering the items listed in **Part A** is the foundation for the full record of conservation. Copies of the preliminary report with the information required in **Part B** should be included with full sets of records.

Separate forms should be used for each window where treatment differs widely. Any change to the original method statement should be noted.

Description of conservation work

Date glass removed .... Date of Reinstatement ....

Conservator/ Name and Address ....
....
....
....
Conservators working on the project ....
....
....
....

Names of academic, scientific or other advisers involved in the
conservation project ....
....
....
....

General Note: When compiling a conservation record, the
conservator should ask whether it would enable someone else
at a later date to tell precisely what work was carried out.

Part B: 1   Removal

Note any further discoveries or observations.

Record the type of material in which the window is set.

Note sizes of pockets and spacing of any previous *ferramenta*
support system discovered in the window mullions and jambs.

Part B: 2   Workshop condition assessment/
Work undertaken

Give a general description of the window, noting details of
specific problems and recording on which panels they occurred.

Give details of previous restorations and note any unusual
features or techniques discovered on the panels (signatures,
glaziers' marks, etc.).

Glass
List types used (muff or crown process, machine drawn etc.).

State condition.

Justify any proposed replacement.

Leading
State condition of existing leading, list sizes and types used.
Note details of any milling marks discovered.

Justify any proposed replacement of existing leading.

List profile and sizes of any new leads inserted. State
manufacturer.

Cleaning
State methods of cleaning and the order of execution.

List any materials used with manufacturer's product reference.

Edge bonding of fractures
List any materials used with manufacturer's product reference.

Plating
State thickness of plate used and whether moulded.

List material used for edge sealing the plated pieces with manufacture product reference.

Paint consolidation
Describe the condition of existing paint.

List any materials used to conserve it with manufacturer's product reference.

Replacement of painted surface
State the name of the artist/painter.

List the manufacturers of any paint, stain and enamels used on the project.

State method of firing, type of kiln and fuel used.

Provide description of any other painting techniques employed.

Note: All new inserted painted glass should be dated and initialled on the piece before installation.

Conservation diagram
Supply three copies of post-conservation diagrams annotated with the symbols detailing work undertaken as indicated on the attached key. If another system is used then please supply a key to this system. The diagram may be a *good* photograph of the annotated full size 'after' rubbing.

Note: Submitted diagrams must be printed large enough to enable them to be read easily.

Part B: 3   Reinstatement

Materials
List composition and ratio of mortar mix or any other materials used for the sealing of the window with their product reference.

List any other relevant materials used during the reinstatement.

Support systems
State size and type of all new support bars used. If existing support system is reused state method of its treatment and provide details of any protective coatings applied.

Environmental and mechanical protective glazing
List all types and sizes of materials used with manufacture product reference of any protective measures taken e.g. wire guards, polycarbonate sheeting, external protective glazing, isothermal glazing etc. Diagrams if applicable should be included.

General
List all other relevant information relating to the reinstatement e.g. condensation trays, opening casements etc.

Part B: 4   Studio photographic documentation

Each panel should be photographed in transmitted light before and after conservation. A panel or panels representing the average condition of the overall window should be selected and photographed additionally in reflected light showing condition of internal and external surfaces before and after conservation. Additional photographs taken during conservation of unusual features, damage, details or discoveries should be included.

Further detailed photographs are welcomed.

All images to be annotated with dedication and location of building, window number, light number, panel number and date, indicating whether before, during or post conservation. (CVMA number system to be applied or drawing with key to support alternative number system).

Four sets of the written and photographic documentation are required. Three sets to be supplied to the CCC and one held by the conservator. Submitted photographs to be of good quality in either colour print or transparency with black and white negatives and contact sheets.

Supply catalogue list of photographs submitted with report with a separate list of additional images that may be held by the conservator.

List of abbreviations to be used on stained glass diagrams

Cracks – Indicate with dotted lines

Ea Edge joined by adhesive – specify in written record

Eb Edge joined by copper foil

L Leaf lead or strap lead

F Artificial filling – specify in written record

P Previous repairs or insertions

Gr Glass installed reversed – specify in written record if previous or new

Gu Re-used glass newly inserted (state source if known)

T Pieces transferred within panel or window (state previous location)

M Modern glass newly inserted

Pi Plated on the front (inside)

Po Plated on the back (outside)

Ps Plated on both sides

If plating is tinted or coloured, 't' may be added.

A New paint pigments (fired)

Newly painted areas are only permitted on plating or new glass. 'A' therefore may be used in conjunction with M, Pi, Po or Ps to denote this application.

Pc Paint consolidation – specify in written record

Please add other symbols if necessary for individual projects.

Note: The purpose of the diagram is to provide factual information on work included in the current programme of conservation, rather than an assessment of the date of every piece of glass in the window. Art historical observations that can be gained only whilst the glass is on the bench should nevertheless be recorded.

The CVMA numbering system

The CVMA numbering system is simple to use and internationally recognized. It obviates the necessity of using lengthy worded descriptions to locate a panel precisely within a building. Although primarily designed for churches, it is based on compass orientation and can be adapted for secular structures. In many cases a building containing historically important window glass will have already been numbered in the archive at the National Monuments Record in Swindon.

CVMA Numbering System for Windows Ground Plan

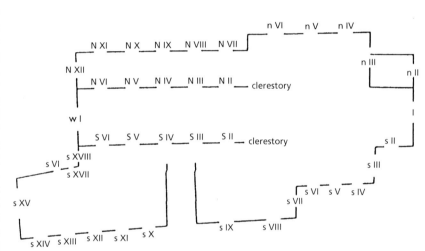

fig. 30
A line is drawn from (liturgical) east to west. The east window is always I, the west wI. Lower case north (= n) and south (= s) are used for all the windows of the relevant orientation above and below the centre line. Nt and St respectively are used for all triforium windows. Upper case is used for all clerestory windows. Roman numerals are used to number each opening from east to west whether or not the window contains historically important glass.

CVMA Numbering System for Windows, Window Plan and Panel Numbering System

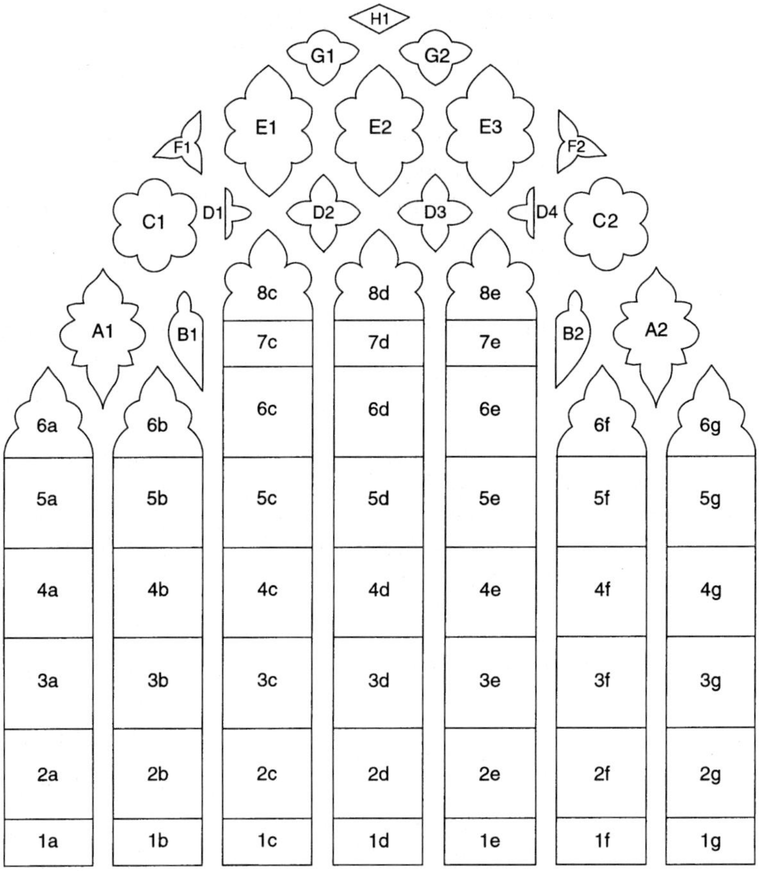

fig. 31
Numbering always follows the same sequence from bottom to top, left to right. In order to distinguish between main light panels and tracery lights, the number precedes the letter for the main lights, the letter comes before the number for the tracery. Both follow a sequential grid pattern directly related to the panel divisions, number of tracery openings and architectural divides. Transom divisions are treated as integral with the panel numberings.

appendix C
Useful addresses and websites

The British Society of Master Glass Painters (BSMGP)

Registered Office
6 Queen Square
London WC1N 3AR
Email: secretary@bsmgp.org.uk
www.bsmgp.org.uk

The national society for all those engaged in stained glass, its manufacture, promotion, conservation, study and appreciation. The society organizes an annual programme of lectures and stained glass activities. It maintains a reference library for members and publishes a regular newsletter and the annual *Journal of Stained Glass*.

The Corpus Vitrearum Medii Aevi (CVMA)

c/o The Courtauld Institute of Art
Somerset House
The Strand
London WC2R 0RN
Tel: 020 7848 1639
Email: Tim.Ayers@courtauld.ac.uk
www.cvma.ac.uk

The Corpus Vitrearum Medii Aevi (Corpus of medieval window glass) is an international project devoted to the study, cataloguing and publication of historic window glass throughout Europe and North America. The British Committee maintains an archive and a website of images.

The Council for the Care of Churches (CCC)

Church House
Great Smith Street
London SW1P 3NZ
Tel: 020 7898 1866
Email: enquiries@ccc.c-of-e.org.uk
www.churchcare.co.uk

For advice on specialist conservators, grant applications and general conservation advice.

English Heritage

23 Savile Row
London W1S 2ET
Tel: 020 7973 3000
Fax: 020 7973 3001
Website:
www.english-heritage.org.uk

English Heritage is the Government's statutory advisory body on conservation issues and policy. It also provides financial assistance and practical advice.

National Association of Decorative and Fine Art Societies (NADFAS)

NADFAS House
8 Guilford Street
London WC1N 1DT
Tel: 020 7430 0730
www.nadfas.org.uk

The NADFAS Church Recorders undertake inventories of church furnishings and fittings.

The National Monuments Record (NMR)

Kemble Drive
Swindon SN2 2GZ
Tel: 01793 414600
Fax: 01793 313606
www.english-heritage.org.uk

The national archive of English Heritage maintains archives concerning historic buildings and archaeological sites and curates the photographic archive of the Corpus Vitrearum Medii Aevi (CVMA).

The Stained Glass Museum

The South Triforium
Ely Cathedral
Ely
Cambridgeshire CB7 4DL
Tel: 01353 660347
Email: stainedgm@lineone.net
www.stainedglassmuseum.org

The only museum in the country devoted exclusively to stained glass.

United Kingdom Institute for Conservation of Historic and Artistic Works (UKIC)

109 The Chandlery
50 Westminster Bridge Road
London SE1 7QY
Tel: 020 7721 8721
Email: ukic@ukic.org.uk
www.ukic.org.uk

The UKIC represents professional and accredited conservators in all disciplines. It maintains a database of accredited conservators.

The Worshipful Company of Glaziers

Glaziers Hall
9 Montague Close
London Bridge
London SE1 9DD
Tel: 020 7403 3300
Fax: 020 7407 6036
Email:
info@worshipfulglaziers.com
www.worshipfulglaziers.com

The modern heir of the medieval craft guild, the Worshipful Company now promotes the contemporary stained glass craft, supports stained glass education and administers a number of national competitions and awards. The Company maintains an information service. Its Glaziers Trust administers small grants towards stained glass conservation.

The photography of stained glass: some guidelines

Any competent amateur photographer can undertake a basic photographic record of the stained glass in a parish church, as long as a few simple guidelines are followed.

Where possible, try to use a single lens reflex (SLR) camera with a range of lenses that will allow you to fill the frame efficiently. A basic 35mm or 50mm lens and a zoom lens of 70mm to 210mm will cover most circumstances.

The use of a tripod is *essential*. Not only does this provide the steady base for the camera during the longer exposures you will need when photographing stained glass, it will also impose a disciplined working method, ensuring a thorough and consistent record. A cable release or timed delayed shutter release will help eliminate any camera vibration. If necessary, position the tripod at some distance from the window in order to avoid steep perspectives and converging verticals.

Avoid direct sunlight. A bright, overcast day is ideal. Turn off all the lights inside the church. Use only transmitted light–turn off your automatic flash, if you have one. Through-the-lens metering is perfectly satisfactory, as it is not usually possible to get close enough to the window to take surface meter readings. If in doubt as to the correct exposure, take several shots at different settings ('bracket' your exposures). As a general rule, choose slower shutter speeds and higher aperture settings (f.11 or higher). For windows of light tone, and where external objects can be seen through the window, choose a lower aperture (f.8 or lower) to ensure that only the glass is in focus.

Slower-rated films should be used. ASA100 is appropriate for most general records. Slower film speeds, i.e. ASA64 and ASA25, can be used by the more experienced. While colour prints are a convenient format and can be labelled easily, colour slides can be projected to any size and can be useful to the conservator. A record in both formats would be ideal. Invest in good quality film in order to ensure an accurate colour balance – ask your film stockist or colour lab for advice.

Plan the compilation of your record carefully. Assign every window in your church a number, marked on a simple ground plan. Distinguish between ground floor and clerestory-level windows. Work around the building systematically. This will allow you to take advantage of the changing lighting conditions during the day. Take a general view and a series of details of each window. Once you have recorded the internal appearance, record the external appearance.

Store your prints, slides and negatives carefully, as all photographic materials deteriorate over time. Cool, dry and dark conditions are best. Make two copies of the record, and store them in different places, to guard against loss or damage. Label prints, negatives and slides, and ensure that the date of the photographic campaign is recorded. A box of unidentified and undated photographs is of limited use. Plan to update your record at intervals, preserving the earlier record for comparative purposes.

Further reading

General

Sarah Brown, *Stained Glass: An Illustrated History*, Studio Editions, London, 1992

Carola Hicks, *Discovering Stained Glass*, Shire Publications, 1996

Medieval stained glass

Sarah Brown, 'Stained glass', in Martin Kemp (ed.), *The Oxford History of Western Art*, Oxford University Press, Oxford, 2000

Sarah Brown and David O'Connor, *Medieval Craftsmen: Glass-Painters*, British Museum Press, London, 1991

Richard Marks, *Stained Glass in England During the Middle Ages*, Routledge & Kegan Paul, London, 1993

The nineteenth century and beyond

Peter Cormack, *The Stained Glass Work of Christopher Whall 1849–1924*, Boston Public Library, Boston, 1999

Martin Harrison, *Victorian Stained Glass*, Barrie & Jenkins, London, 1980

Conservation

Articles on protective glazing in *Newsletter of the Centre International du Vitrail* 41/42, 1998 Switzerland.

Keith Barley, 'Stained glass', in *Treasures on Earth. A Good Housekeeping Guide to Churches and their Contents*, Donhead Publishing, London, 1994

Sandra Davidson, and Roy Newton, *The Conservation of Glass*, Butterworth Heineman, London, 1989

Norman H. Tennant, (ed.) *The Conservation of Glass and Ceramics: Research, Practice and Training*, James & James, London, 1999

Photography of stained glass

Richard Brun, *A Guide to the Photography of Church Furnishings*, Church House Publishing, London 1999

Terry Buchanan, 'The photography of stained glass', in *The Journal of Stained Glass*, XVIII, No. 3 (1988), pp. 308–13

Index

Page numbers in *italic figures* refer to illustrations. Churches are indexed under the place where they are located.

Index